VIOLADES &
APPLEDOWN

George Messo

Violades
&
Appledown

POEMS

Shearsman Books

First published in the United Kingdom in 2012 by
Shearsman Books
50 Westons Hill Drive
Emersons Green
Bristol
BS16 7DF

Shearsman Books Ltd Registered Office
30–31 St. James Place, Mangotsfield, Bristol BS16 9JB
(this address not for correspondence)

www.shearsman.com

ISBN 978-1-84861-264-8

Acknowledgements
The author wishes to thank the editors of the
following publications, blogs and online sites where
these poems originally appeared:

Andy Brown Poetry (Blogspot): 'Winter. Fox and Hawk,' 'Morning at
Midnight.'

Conversation Papers: 'Flighten'

Damazine: 'Kingfisher at Seven Lakes'

Poetry Salzburg Review: 'Questions at Rize Fort,' 'Fishbones,'
'Noncompush'

The Raconteur: 'The Unremarkable Life of Ponds'

Shadow Train: 'The Barbel of Zurich'

Shearsman: 'Aligned Underfoot,' 'The Chart Room of Abu
Bashaar'

Turkish Book Review: 'Violades and Appledown,' 'Fishbones'

Contents

ONE: *Distances*

TWO: *I Said He Said*

THREE: *Otherlike*

FOUR: *Fishbones*

To Peter Didsbury

ONE

Distances

Questions at Rize Fort

Have you noticed in poems about woods,
or forests, or the places shadows gather
and swell, how species start to talk
only when the humans have gone?

Who remembers the mystery mirrored
in the dew-cupped leaf moments
before it falls and spins through
the dusty half-light at dusk?

There are journeys back through
tangled woods, all glottal stops
then weird peripatetic syntax.
What the hell could it possibly mean?

According to what we ourselves have seen,
said the dragonfly shortly after I'd left,
there are moments lived only once
when a second's pause decides everything.

Crossing the Pass

I

When Tu Fu sat on the west
wall of his hut in Brocade city

wrapped in mulberry leaves and
saw a shaft of young wheat erect

in river fields begin to sway he
wondered first how long he had

and if he'd see this world again.
But he'd never seen Zigana.

II

In the classical Chinese of Tu Fu
the character *ts'ung* meaning

to follow or *hence* shows one
man following another.

Those days folk believed
pearls were mermaid's tears.

Tu Fu placed one in a box
to pay his tax which later

turned to blood. He wrote
his poems in red, inspired

by rising winds and tax.

III

A butterfly dreamt it was Tu Fu.
In the approximate centre of his reverie

—for a butterfly dreams from back to front
and in a sequence of three halves—

Tu Fu falls asleep in a melon patch
and dreams he is a butterfly.

IV

Cottage smoke over limpid *Kızılırmak*,
Red River. The Catfish sweat-out

thoughts like pearls, blood-wisdom.
Pitiable fate, to guide the taxman's boat.

A Tea Bowl

for Michael Hillard

Drink jewel-drops, master Kampaku.

Think *temmoku* of the black-glazed bowl,

your golden lip, floating in blue-dark spots

of a vessel made for tea.

Downpaths

from Bashō

Sunlight—its slow ascent
rising through orchard-apple scent.

Aligned Underfoot

In those days, your best poems
lived under bridges, in wild garlic;

tiny constellations dreaming out
from lost rings of darkness. Well,

there must have been other things too.
There were: flowers —small & white—

but precisely who was reading
that *Book of Brilliance*, I don't know.

Go back a little, I missed something
—it's all shade but there is a place

darker, deeper than the rest, where
earth is always bare, perpetually dry,

where nothing grows, nothing could,
a perfect *where* to hide: your enemies,

yourself, a treasure.

Uqair

Sun over sheet-metal bay.
The fish are in their drum.

Tap tap tap they sign
to us through blue

forgetfulness, a skirl
of clicking reels.

*

The Arab fleets
who sailed from here

brought
from the East

salinity
baked in amber.

*

Hagool, the needlefish.
Canad, the mackerel.

On springtide leatherbacks.
On neaptides gander,

cormorant, and weed
bowel-rank from the sea.

Villish

Unreachable ruin of stars.
Look out across the village,

open doors and go out.
There is work to be done.

Dog-frost mauling your feet
quickens you over fields,

through rusted gates, to the skirt of Han Farm Hill.
Ice about your eyes is thickening now—

O look!
Stars in their fixed abodes are settling here.

Climb. Build all you can of word and deed.
Ascend, as the sleeping village sleeps on.

Zigana Mountain Poem

Moved one step
into that crack & snap
of dry twigs, needles

brown, yellow-green, heard,
and the nerve-skin quivers.
Only now, they run.

Kingfisher at Seven Lakes

I

In his time sufi divine
Beytullah Ferit Efendi
slept under bridges, in ditches,
on beds of stitchweed & whortle;

his clothes were made of sack,
a mud-thwacked, rat-eaten mass,
but a man lived beneath
this mantle of stink & filth:

Beytullah Ferit Efendi.

II

Crystal-wire, scattering light,
let's call it a river
held in air over schist:
cataracts heard a mile away.

III

Beytullah Ferit Efendi,
the ever never-changing
sufi divine: a waterfall,
its turbid pool, a minnow
wetting the kingfisher's gullet.

Fat Heart Upload

With care, there are things
we can still be happy about,
lulled by the coma TV

into numbness so like a
thought that thinks you're
only half alive, the pain-

ful part chopped out.
How wrong you are
especially

when you're right.
Long ago, in a town
called Austin's Ferry

I was a different man
each morning but the same
man at night: thoughtless,

happy, with gatherings
of mysterious garlands
and pity to wreath me in,

alone and drunk and
hauling my cares,
heavy but easily changed.

A Chorus of Djinns Sings on Hickory Day

The barren winter field was glass imperishable, a frost-
locked lattice door, when at last warmth set its key
in uncommon cloudlessness; a halting world was lost.

We slipped on boots, trudged its ruts and furrows thawing
in that opened light. And the sayable tree
shook its unshakable flesh, waving us on; each cloying

squelch and earth-fart marked our step. Our short memory
of opulent fields, of the power-gods whose lesson in modesty
taught impermanence: all we shall ever know of history.

Starburn Blister

All day I've been thinking: *The past is a goner*
but still there are paths

into an unreconstructed past
of tall grass and bog cotton,

over the Stinchar bridge
and the forest road to Loch Braden.

*

All day I've been saying: *Purple Moor Grass*,
decanting its syllables into a half-filled memory.

But we know the need to forget.
Soon the road begins to slow and there

an almost imperceptible rise draws you up
to its brow. It's then you'll see Loch Braden.

Words for a Wishing Well

There is a silence so profound
at the heart of all sound

but let me tell you this—

a stone tossed down a well
descends into a hell

of noise we can only guess.

Distances

At low tide sand softens and is almost mud.
From here you can wade to the island
the shallow bay boulder pocked; a chalky
tide line sights you through morning mist.
What pulls you time-bound back again
but something recognized? A foghorn pulsing
over the bay, says *here* and *here* and *here*.

A washed-up wooden crate from Jaffa,
though you cannot really say, how it came
to where a scarf of wrackweed oil black
wraps the coastline's craned neck,
what once apart from salted air it might have packed.

Forgetfilled and Thoughtless

Each one barely differs
from the last, but note and mark
and know their partial gaze—

shadows cast to spook and put me down.
Stay tucked and tight: all forearms, smooth
strokes, nothing jarred or ragged.

At Cole's the summer weed
will rise and fall with fingers,
all invisible holds and snags

as light breaks across your bow
and oars dip to press
from blades their tiny gathering shards.

The Barbel of Zurich

Yet there you are

and the air we breathe
diverse and separately so

sounds nothing to you
of me. But sensing

you I slow my breath
to whisper now across

your glass-like sleeve
and there you go

muscle pulsing
into glides,

into currents,
into crowds.

TWO

I Said He Said

(David Vogel 1891–1944)

Less Happy If You Were

for Kelvin Corcoran

When crows pecked out your eyes, we knew,
David Vogel, they'd sing *This World Awakes To Silence*
in such—excuse the pun—impeccably lilting Hebrew.

We applaud the learning and syntax of birds
but who remembers you, David Vogel, beneath
your blanket of sound. Even silence observes

its minute for you but not the crow, who goes:
*In the dark I look within and find there
only a void to sing* and like the night it flows

slowly from infinity to far away, from far away
to himself, David Vogel, resting in silence,
eyeless, waking, far from the labour of his day.

He Said

I stood in that vast silence, he said, as if
it were fluid seeping or a wound I could not
staunch with words. He spoke again, as if

the picture were a dark hole consuming him,
the tongue of a bell striking nothing. Shoes
with nowhere to go; their worn slim

soles soundless on the tiled floor, too light,
he said, to creek a wooden board. Up
to his neck in them and slowly losing sight

of the mute bell sounding empty space, as if
it were some unattainable but shocking
metaphor or simile of glasses and false teeth

in search of mouths or a pyramid of eyes.
In that roaring deafness, he said, my heart
was a bird's pulse, moments before it dies.

Birdbone Blue

The dead know nothing, he said, but dream forever
in old dialects. Heavy, unwieldy tongues
which rise and fall, breaking the wren's back if ever

they sing it to life. My childhood, he said,
was a field, a hedgerow, drains and reeds, ponds
and marshes, seldom trees. I came to recognize

even there, a silence so breathless its rush
to speak blew me flat, face down on wet fields.
After years I would rise from there made of clay,

my chest a cuneiform script not even I could
understand. Out of clay, he said,
the words we take them for: *blackbird*, *oriole*, *crow*.

Morning at Midnight

A moment ago is a marvellous way to make a memory,
of a past so recently here like a lingering scent
or a body-shape left on a bed, she said. Our history

says *once* and means *in a time not now*; reticent
but faithful to your fragile need for mystery.

*

When the time is right we find what's absent
—or does it find us?—tucked surreptitiously
where it's least sought: the past in the present.

Enduring but reducible. That, she said, is the poverty
of life in a present where the future's already spent.

I Said He Said

Your mountains are empty promises, he said,
and folding them into a perfect square

handed them back to me. The Tao is nowhere
to be found, he said, yet nourishes

and completes all things. Umm, I said,
chewing my lip, unfolding Orange Drop Peak.

Nowhere, I said, is a mountain waiting to be found.
Exhausting steps will nourish you, I lied;

the summit will clothe you in rags; your need
complete, blisters will float you home;

your body will sing its everything;
your hands will unlearn through touch.

I said, he said, mountains are empty *premises*.
Umm, I said. Umm.

The Unremarkable Life of Ponds

When Ponds entered the ditch he thought
how different it was from his bed
but a fine place nonetheless to rest,
and taking out his pocket watch
he checked the time, loosened his tie
and lay wide-eyed in the dry groove
of the ditch. Night was a long way off.

At precisely eight twenty-two and five
seconds, Ponds lay down in the ditch
staring up and out at a perfectly blue sky.
A bird might have passed but didn't.
It was winter and threads of warm breath
trailed and waved around him.
It was now eight twenty-three, exactly.

Ponds had several thoughts and the first
trilled like the Lydian scale on a dulcimer.
The second twitched like a knotted sack
of kittens falling into a dark lake.
We shall never know which was which.
One of them said, a water-drop falls so far
it evaporates before it reaches the ground

and you, Mister Ponds, are a water-drop.
The other one said, perfection is a terrible delusion.
Go home, while the heart still pumps
its forward space, but time moves back. And Ponds
rose from the frozen earth, climbed out
of the dry ditch and reversed across the winter
field. It was then remarkably eight o'clock.

At the edge of each momentous event the air
thins and drops away into a soundless chasm,
or a ditch.
What hope is there for Ponds, once it is clear
he will never go on, crossing his winter field,
his amber warmth erase each perishable step,
turn back through time, still his trembling

shadow in the morning light and be at peace?
Like many great thoughts, this one leads to nothing
but Ponds, standing by his wooden fence, going in
or coming out of the long undying dawn.
There are parts of our lives we put to one side
and then forget, scattered and dimmed in their own
bruised darkness, hard to define but definite.

Like Ponds, standing in the feathery dawn,
his right hand reaching for the curtain of cold air
he'll draw apart, finally stepping into fate,
burdened and heedless of consequence, one who
believes there is something before there is anything,
whose life can never speak for what is invisible in ours,
even as the minute-hand turns on his pocket watch.

Don't Fall Asleep Now

When surgeons pried you apart like a tin of sardines,
wrists deep in that wild meat,
your heart blew bubbles in its own blood.

Wake up, you said, as we turned to the lake shore.
Mountains hung above us.
We're almost there, you said.

Flighten

First we thought it was just a violent landing.
But then we suddenly descended and there was impact.
We suddenly found ourselves in a field.

Tuncer Mutlucan

Sometimes it happens, as if, she said, you didn't know,
under cold cliffs air like grace on needy flesh,
weightless and cool, rises in playful circles from below:

unfolding, half-formed, vanishing into thinness.
Discrete truths cluster among themselves,
knowable, but then without use or purpose.

Sometimes, she said, it is better to fall and, falling,
thank no one. Circle the ancient wood. Do you
see? A place to land? Forget about dying.

Throw off your soul. Do not be taken in or yield
to illusions of flight, or this very peculiar surprise
on suddenly finding yourself in a field...

Their Very Adherents

I'll rest in this silence, she said.
I knew they were not her words
but David's and the blue child
in him nourished on solitude.

There are many silences, she said
and soundlessness is only one.
We've been there but never returned.
For David it was home, of sorts.

David Vogel, do you hear us
breaking through the mirror
of your black, marble pool?
Can you feel us from within

your perfect cube of darkness
cut from lamplight and flame?
It's useless, she said, to think
of the soul as a season.

David always wanted spring.
It's pointless, she said, to seek
in the shadow of trees whispers
of a man unfolding like a leaf.

THREE

Otherlike

(Scenes from
The David Collection,
Copenhagen)

Like and Otherlike Words

Like and otherlike words
that finger mouths
—say *deliquat*
made from *crazysmall*—
are often cherry-round,
sour-juiced, but drive
a path across the tongue
like sherbet, otherlike
sweet; nebulae
built of air, a sense-city
squeezed from individual
sound: you, *deliquat*.
You, sour-sweet *crazysmall*.

The Curious Thing:
A Dissertation

In *Iskandar Contemplating the Sirens*, fourteen sixty three, the crowned head peering from behind a cloud-like nimbus of rock, and gazing squint-eyed through an oil-black stream filled with voluptuous nymphs, is none other than Alexander the Great.

'Voluptuous' is surely stretching it. They are, after all, thumb-sized caricatures in human form. But putting all else aside, the curious thing—for what is more natural than a landscape of bathing nymphs—is Alexander himself, double-headed, each cranium circled in gold.

The eyes look left. The eyes look right. To the head facing right a finger is held to a lip. It is a finger of surprise and invitation, pointing to a mouth and the tongue therein: Alexander's great organ of seduction. And in this moment of conjuring and complicity it is through these very eyes we share their owner's view of the nymphs: androgynous, supine, wet with readiness.

In this triangulated view, however, there is yet a fourth point, hovering as it were like the invisible apex of a pyramid.

Remarkable Happens

In early November 1432
seated on his throne
a silent world of courtier,
camel, horse and ox,
dumbstruck and pale
as Djamshid is carried
into the air by demons.

Beheaded

When Müjdee ran
head cocked high
the plump apple of his throat
full ripe with all that he would say

into the waiting sword
of Grand Vizier Harun
did he still believe his god
would trip him up

and in those vital seconds
falling from his life
avoid its sharpened truth?

Poor fool,
his tiny head
mouthing breathless Os
across at his quivering body.

FOUR

Fishbones

Fishbones

for Andrew Loader

I'm not a place, I'm a person, she said,
and taking up her atolls, her archipelagos,
she promptly packed and left. But instead

of the customary questions and recriminations
I sided with her immediately. True enough,
no island is its own man. Imagination's

better half can sometimes tilt its heavy head
and wink, as if to say: "That's the way!"
And I'd be off at a trot wherever it led.

And if a woman suddenly appeared on a beach
I'd think myself into her grain, my delirious
eagerness, as always, sliding beyond reach

of my own human heart, a place of constant
gains and retreat, like sea to that very beach
at night, swollen, invisible to its silent want.

A Jellied Pig's Head

after Günter Grass

Cut a pig's head vertically in two
leaving an eye, a cheek, the warren
of its ear, left or right, half a snout,
the bowl of its brain, its sawn off jaw;

two of the trotters should be split
taking care to remove the disk of skin
with the blue inspection stamp;
then take a large bay leaf, an onion

studded with cloves, a sprinkling of mustard
seed no bigger than a child's clenched fist
and place them in boiling water, salted,
with a levelled tablespoon of modest rage;

be sure there is just enough water
to cover each part, and position
the ear flap on top so it won't
stick to the bottom and burn.

Boil gently for an hour or more, but
don't forget that after a while
a certain scum will start to rise:
tiny vein excretions, snout puss, earwax,

a brownish brain-bit frothy brawn.
It's better to scoop this off and reduce
to a pure, mildly savoury broth,
stirring vigorously from the start—

what volatile rage there is will curdled
with the froth and is easily congealed
into protest. Meanwhile, chop onions,
two apples, peeled and cored, preferably small.

Dice gherkins into tiny cubes, grind
pepper in your mind as though it were
a mortar; add ginger root, grated lemon,
and leave your impotent rage to simmer.

Take a tentative jab at the cheek—
when the meat is soft, the back teeth
loose in their gums but rooted still,
and those parts prone to oozing gristley

fat peel off around the jellied edge of trotters,
and the split skin around the ear,
then, lift everything out of the pot:
the bay leaf, the onion studded with cloves;

use a ladle to search for splintered bone,
for the front teeth easily dislodged,
for the sand-like grains removed from the ear.
Leave the broth to simmer over a low heat

and place the rest on a plate to cool
with a kitchen window open wide, your eyes
narrowed so the pupils contract.
Proceed with detaching the softer parts

of the snout, the cheek, the layers of flesh
beneath the bones and skin. Better not
leave the gristle, soft and firm, or the
jellied bits of the ear just under the skin;

scrape them off with the back of a knife
since it's these, the lamellated gums,
the horny tongue rooting down the windpipe,
the oesophagus, and no other parts of the pig

that impart their special, passionate taste
to the brawny broth. Do not fail
to let greasy fingers drip dry over steam
rising from the pot, for, in this way

it aids the process of natural gelling—
which is what our pig's head will do:
set naturally, without gelatine or power,
communicating, as best it can, its jellied rage.

Then, place all the parts previously removed
back into the broth—that's to say,
the meat and fat, the gristle, together
with the onions and apples, the cubed gherkins,

the pounded pepper too. Stir in a spoonful
of tarragon vinegar, according to taste.
Don't be too sparing because vinegar
loosens its tang when chilled. Bring

the whole thing to the boil once more,
adding now the perfectly thickened rage,
which has been simmering on the side
and can now be safely poured

into a stoneware dish, freshly rinsed,
which should be carefully set in a cool,
draughty place in readiness for the next
night's well-disposed guests, who will

appreciate a nicely prepared jellied pig's head.
And nothing need go to waste, for the coarse
trotters, the gristle and bone, can be cooled
again with a fistful of spice, provided

enough rage can still be found in the house.
And in this way, with turnips and barley
and other such miseries for tiny mouths,
a simple, nutritious meal can be made.

i.m. Michael Hamburger 1924—2007

Folkone: A Song

Few know the cost of land in human blood,
know the depths of sluices, the width of drains
and dykes; the bone-parting, ball-crunching pains
of farmhands working the neighbourhood.

But that was my father, one whose death
even then was slowly forcing the light,
staking its claim, asserting its right
to speak its one unutterable shibboleth.

New Holland. When he finally said it,
gave a name to the rank shit-pit
from which we crawled, a family unfit
for any other name but *Leech*, he'd spit

the after-slime off his tongue. Bitter
to his dying breath; hated his life, himself,
his dog, loved his wife but beat her,
hated his kids, hated fucking hate itself.

Few know the cost of land in human blood...
...

But that was my father, who even in death
spoke always of a land he'd left, spoke
through his sodden sluice-tide breath,
words invisible, impossible to revoke.

The Chart Room of Abu Bashaar

Before the sun is even up
forests are on the move.

Sailing through milk fat pasture,
there is a scraping of bark,

a scoring of hulls on hobbled earth.
And from where I'm at

I'm willing to consider their pine flotilla
a refuge for my long self-pity.

Down the valley we go! Let's drink
from the tears of crushed leaves,

anoint our brows with globes of sap.
Set each man to his mast

and each branch to its purpose.
Can there really be a thing more extraordinary

than the terrible rib-cracking roar
of a valley clearing its throat?

Lay down our position, Master Lee,
twenty degrees to the east

where already the climbing dial
illumines our edge and end.

Into whatever abyss it rises from
we throw ourselves like tinder

into a furnace. Each man to his mast!
And me to my self-pity.

Sticky Peaches

*You'll find a slight squeeze on the
hooter an excellent safety precaution,
Miss Scrumptious.*
— Caractacus Potts

A sticky peach invites
surprise, oral celebrations;
trickles and drips and
tongue-tied sexual teasing.
Caress the wizen skin

of a week-old peach—
do your fingers want
to linger in its fragile tucks
and folds, tacky with
residue? Mine do.

Then try a sticky peach—
just when the nectar's
tartness is turning sweet.

The old will outlive us.
And although the young
are too numerous to count
we already have plans
to forget them.

Violades & Appledown

Is there anyone better than you,
before poetry finally empties the room

to sing us back to our own lives,
bitten, half-wild, living simply,

when the triumph of dawn too
empties us back into words, words

without language. Your song
is the need I'll settle for:

cold water fresh from its well.

Noncompush

for Chris Milton

One day, rising early from a restless sleep,
I dressed, wet my face, and walked out
on my past, into an empty street, to Ulus

where I boarded a train for Kars. I have
never been to Kars, before or since: a hole
never to be filled but often fallen through.

I sat in the cold belly of a train while
Anatolia and its towns like spilt milk
happened in the snow-bound world outside.

I wrote my name on a window and then
I wrote yours. Soon after, everything dimmed.
"Where are you going?" they asked.

Kars was a long way off. "Kayseri" I said,
and reading again my name on the glass,
I remembered who I was and got off.

Therefore

I. Sleep Was a Stranger

It is Spring, seventeen seventy-five.
A boy named Wapoos, barely alive,
walks to the settlement. It is clear
he has come a long way. From where,
who knows? Minute examination
shows no gun, no ammunition.
Moments before, he's seen climbing
a lofty tree—pine perhaps—stowing
his bag of provisions. A stranger
here, he is, therefore, a danger
before he is anything. Conjecture,
most barbed of all rumour,
says he met and killed a man;
the meat in his bag is human.

II.   Skipertogan

...he gave freely what it was not in his power to protect.
Samuel Hearne

Fresh breeze and flying showers found us on the fourth.
I'll write a little now, for what it's worth,

of moss fires, simple meals, a diet of raw venison.
Jackasheypuck blunts the stabbing air's sharp reason

and makes best of intolerable cold, company
enough, with *wishacumpuckey* (used for tea).

Moss, be it sphagnum or not, will swell in rain
like a sponge and can't be lit. Therefore, retain

a few dried fragments, tucked in your skipertogan.
Imagine, if you can, the skipertogan:

a pocketful of sparks, the miraculous
warmth, a single spell against darkness.

Winter. Fox and Hawk

for Tina Peace

Frequently near, the summer months pass
and even here we speak so often of you

now, coming like a spirit these years
as the short-winged hawk, too light

to lift his kill, rests by the frozen river.
I have carried you, and brought you to this

far cold north, through moveable snow,
bewildered. You were my *poowogan*,

dream walker, soft-footed, while I,
mute and dumbed-down by frost,

whitened beyond my age by rime,
stalked you through aspen, willow and pine.

And here, where forest entrails spill
into winter light, you find me, straying

out from the forest's dark memory:
your racing heart, heat to my tongue.

What Kenny Would Say

for Kenny Fountain

A last walk in brittle light
through acacia dwarf oleander

and the bowls of discarded cement,
chipped and broken brick

marking the city's edge.
You build a house of the past

and live in it. I dig
a hole and cover it.

Where else could we be,
our future need

close but anonymous?
Say whatever you will,

night is a cupped hand over us.
Let's walk to the top of the hill.

Notes

A Tea Bowl
Temmoku glaze with silver spots. Jian Ware. Southern Song dynasty, 12th—13th century. 12.2cm in diameter. In *Ceramics from China, Korea and Japan: Selected Treasures from The Museum of Oriental Ceramics*, Osaka, Japan.

Uqair
Today Uqair is a tiny, remote fishing village on the east coast of Saudi Arabia, consisting of two or three dwellings and dominated by an ancient fort. It is believed the Arab/Islamic fleets sailed from here on missions of trade and conquest to India, Indonesia and Malaysia. The Danish archaeologist Geoffrey Bibby tried to link Uqair to the lost ancient city of Gerrha.

A Chorus of Djinns Sings On Hickory Day
The last sentence borrows from George Roux's *Ancient Iraq*, Penguin Books, 1964.

Less Happy If You Were
David Vogel (1891–1944) was an itinerant Russian-born Hebrew poet who, it is believed, died in Auschwitz. His poem, *This World Awakes To Silence*, is translated by Peter Everwine and is included in Everwine's *From The Meadow: Selected and New Poems*, University of Pittsburgh Press, 2004. David Vogel appears frequently and variously throughout the poems in Part Two: *I Said He Said*.

Flighten
Tuncer Mutlucan, survivor. Flight TK1951 crashed at 10.31am on 25 February, 2009, shortly before arrival at Schiphol Airport, Amsterdam. Reported in *The Times*, 26.02.09.

The Curious Thing: A Dissertation
All of the poems in Part Three respond in various ways to Islamic miniatures held in *The David Collection* at Kronprinsessegade 30, Copenhagen. See also Kjeld von Folsach's *For The Privileged Few: Islamic Miniature Painting From The David Collection*, Louisiana Museum of Modern Art, 2007.

A Jellied Pig's Head
My version has its source in the late Michael Hamburger's translation of the German original, in *Poems of Günter Grass*, Penguin Books, 1969.

Noncompush
"My brother is little better than noncompush. He would give away his shirt off his back, and the teeth out of his head; nay, as for that matter, he would have ruinated the family with his ridiculous charities..." Tobias Smollett, in *The Expedition of Humphrey Clinker*, 1771.

Therefore
For Part I, reference to events in *Sleep Was A Stranger* can be found in Samuel Hearne's *A Journey to the Northern Ocean*, 1795, a classic of early Canadian history and exploration. For Part II, Hearne writes: "Skipertogan is a small bag that contains a flint and steel, also a pipe and tobacco, as well as touchwood, etc. for making a fire." Of *Jackasheypuck* he gives this full description: "This herb much resembles Creeping Box, and is only used, either by the Indians or English, to mix with tobacco, which makes it smoke mild and pleasant, and would, I am persuaded, be very acceptable to many smokers in England." *Wishacumpuckey* (or Wee-sa-ca-pucca or Wish-a-ca-pucca), according to Hearne, "grows in most parts of this country" and "is said by some Authors to have great medical virtues, applied, either inwardly as an alterative, or outwardly dried and pulverized, to old sores and gangrenes... It is, however, much used by the lower class of the Company's servants as tea; and by some thought very pleasant."

Winter. Fox And Hawk
In the writings of David Thompson (1770—1857), one of the most important surveyors of North America, the author writes: "Every man believes, or wishes to believe, he has a familiar being, who takes care of him, and warns him of danger, and other matters which otherwise he could not know; this imaginary being he calls his *Poo wog gan*..." In his footnote to Thompson's remark, William E. Moreau adds that in Cree cosmology the "*pawakan* is the dream visitor who appears during the puberty vision fast and is regarded as a lifelong personal guardian, guide,

and counsellor." See *The Writings of David Thompson, Volume 1, The Travels, 1850 Version*, edited by William E. Moreau, McGill–Queen's University Press, Montreal, Canada. 2009. P.107.